I haven't got a Clou!

POCKET DICTIONARY OF FRENCH BUILDING TERMS

I haven't got a Clou!

POCKET DICTIONARY OF FRENCH BUILDING TERMS

Eileen Carey

Eileen Carey
2014

First Printing: 2014

ISBN 978-1-291-83514-4

Published by Eileen Carey

62990 France

www.frenchdiytranslations.co.uk

To my dear family who have always believed in me, and without whose patient help and input this book would never have been realised.

Contents

Acknowledgements

I would like to extend a big thank you to digital designer Richard Kelly, who has given me support and technical assistance in the production of the book cover and my website. You can visit Richard's site at www.richardkelly.me.uk

Introduction

I put this book together because as a frequent visitor to the DIY stores in France I, like many others, have struggled with the translations for certain tools and materials and the fact that the same items can change their names from department to department....

Although it could be fun and much laughter was had, I felt frustrated and inadequate on my missions.

So here we have it ... it is not a heavy duty manual, it is just something light to carry with you to the DIY stores, quincailleries and the like. Hopefully it might just get you out of a predicament!

You will see that it has been grouped into departments as well as alphabetically. This means that items which are often used together can be found within the same section.

Bon Courage!

BATHROOM ACCESSORIES
ACCESSOIRE DE SALLE DE BAIN

Duck board	Caillebotis
Mirror illuminated	Miroir éclairant
Pedal bin	Poubelle à pédale
Shower curtain	Rideau de douche
Toilet brush holder	Pot à balai
Toilet roll holder	Dérouleur de papier WC
Toilet seat	Abattant WC
Towel rail	Porte-serviette

BATHROOM FITTINGS
APPAREIL SANITAIRE

Bath	Baignoire
Bathroom cabinet	Meuble de salle de bain
Bathroom panel	Tablier
Cistern	Réservoir
Hand basin	Lave-main
Jacuzzi bath	Baignoire balnéo
Macerater	Broyeur
Mixer tap single lever	Mitigeur
Mixer tap twin tap	Mélangeur
Pivoting door	Porte pivotante

Shower	Douche
Shower enclosure	Parois de douche
Shower kit	Ensemble de douche
Shower tray	Receveur de douche
Sliding door	Porte coulissante
Tap	Robinet
Toilet	Toilette
Toilet bowl	Cuvette WC
Wall hung WC	WC suspendu
Wash basin/stand	Lavabo
Wash bowl	Vasque

BUILDING MATERIALS
MATÉRIAUX DE CHANTIER

Ballast	**Gravier**
Bitumen	**Bitume**
Blocks concrete insulation	**Parpaing** brique alvéolaire
lightweight	béton cellulaire
Cement	**Ciment**
Concrete mixer	**Bétonnière**
Corrugated sheets	**Plaques ondulées**
bitumen	bitumée
galvanised	galvanisée
synthetic fibre	fibre synthétique
Damp proof membrane	**Film sous dalle**

Expansion joints	Joint de dilatation
Filler	Enduit de rebouchage
Flashing/lead	Bande de plomb
Mortar	Mortier
Plasticiser	Résine latex
Polycarbonate	Plaques roofing polycarbonate
Props	Étais
Reinforcing rods	Fer à béton
Sand	Sable
Scaffolding	Échafaudage
Trestle	Tréteau
Wheel barrow	Brouette

CENTRAL HEATING
CHAUFFAGE CENTRAL

Bleed valve	Purgeur d'air

Boiler
  fuel
  gas
	Chaudière
	fioul
	gaz

Expansion vessel	Vase d'expansion
Heated towel rail	Sèche-serviette
Pump	Circulateur

Radiator
  manual valve
  thermostatic
	Radiateur
	robinet simple
	thermostatique

DOORS
PORTES

Door & frame	Bloc-porte
Exterior door	Porte d'entrée
Folding door	Porte pliante
Internal door	Porte intérieure
Lifting door	Porte basculante
Mortice lock	Serrure à mortaiser
Motorised	Motorisée
Service door	Porte de service
Sliding door	Porte coulissante

DRAINAGE
ÉVACUATION

Bend	**Coude**
Downpipe	**Tuyau de descente**
Drain rod	**Déboucheur canalisation**
Grease separator	**Séparateur à graisse**
Gutter	**Gouttière**
Gutter clip	**Crochet de gouttière**
Gutter guard	**Crapaudine**
Inspection chamber	**Regard**
Joint	**Jonction**
Pipe clip	**Collier**

Septic tank	Fosse septique
Stop end	Fond gouttière
Straight connector	Manchon

ELECTRICAL
ÉLECTRICITÉ

Aerial	Antenne
Air conditioning	Climatisation
Backing box	Boîte d'encastrement
plaster board wall	boîte plaque de plâtre
solid wall	boîte à sceller
Battery	Pile
Battery charger	Chargeur de pile
Bulb	Ampoule
Bulb holder	Douille
Cable	Câble
rigid	rigide
flexible	souple
Circuit breaker	Coup-circuit

Conduit	Gaine
Connecting strip	Barrette de connnexion
Convector	Convecteur
Cooker hood	Hotte de cuisine
Electric heating	Chauffage électrique
Electric radiator	Panneau rayonnant
Extension cable	Rallonge
Extension lead	Enrouler de câble
Extension socket (anti surge)	Bloc parafoudre
Fan ventilation	Aérateur
Free-standing heaters	Chauffage d'appoint

Fuse box	Tableau électrique
Heated towel rail	Séche-serviette
Insulating tape	Ruban isolant
Junction box	Boîte de derivation
Oil filled radiator	Radiateur chaleur douce à fluide
Plug	Prise de courant
two pin	fiche mâle
Satellite dish	Antenne parabolique
Socket	Prise
extension socket	fiche femelle
Socket waterproof	Prise étanche
Strip light	Réglette

Switch	Interrupteur
Switch (two way)	Va-et-vient
Test meter	Appareil de mesure
Thermostat	Thermostat
Vent	Grille d'aération
Ventilator unit	VMC (ventilation mécanique contrôle)
Wire	Fil

FIREPLACES
CHEMINÉES

Air vent	Grilles d'aération
Chimney pipe	Tuyau de cheminée
Chimney sweep kit	Kit ramonage
Fire guard	Pare-feu
Stove built in	Foyer/Insert
Stove free-standing	Poêle à bois
Wood fire	Feu de bois

FLOOR COVERING
REVÊTEMENTS DE SOL

Carpet	Moquette
Clip system	Clipser
Door bars	Barre de seuil
Double sided tape	Double face bande
Edge bar	Barre d'arrêt
Finished flooring	Parquet
Floorboard	Plancher
Flooring ratchet strap	Sangle de serrage
Glue	Colle
Junction strip	Barre de jonction
Laminate	Sol stratifié

Lino	Linoleum
Nail	Clou
Skirting board	Plinthe
Underlay	Sous-couche

INSULATION
ISOLATION

Draught excluder	Isolation thermique
Fibre glass	Laine de verre
Plaster board	Plaques de plâtre
Rockwool	Laine de roche
thick	épaisse
thin	mince
Sound insulation	Isolation phonique
Vermiculite	Vermiculite

INTERIOR WALLS
CLOISONS

Ceiling rail	Fourrure
Filler	Enduit joint
Glass blocks	Briques de verre
Jointing tape	Bande pour joints
Metal stud frame	Rail de cloisons
Plaster	Plâtre
Plaster board screws	Vis plaque de plâtre
Plaster board waterproof	Plaque de plâtre hydrofuge
Profile	Profil
Vertical wall rail	Montant

IRONMONGERS
QUINCAILLERIE

Angle bracket	Équerre d'assemblage
Blinds	Stores
Bolt	Boulon
Bungee	Sandow
Cable/steel	Câble acier
Cable tensioner	Tendeur oeil/crochet
Chain	Chaîne
Clip	Mousqueton
Crowbar	Pince à decoffrer
Curtain rod	Barre à rideaux

Door stop	Butée de porte
Drain rod	Déboucheur canalisation
Drawing pin	Punaise
Dustbin	Poubelle
Foot scraper	Caillebotis
Handles	Poignées
Hinge	Charnière
Hook	Crochet
Hose	Tuyau
Hose reel	Dévidoir
Jerrycan	Jerrycan
Jet head	Lance à jet
Jubilee clip	Collier de serrage

Key	Clé
Letter box	Boîte aux lettres
Lock	Verrou
Lubricants	Lubrifiantes
Metal sheeting	Plaque métal
Mortice lock	Serrure à mortaiser
Moulding	Moulure
Nail	Clou
Nozzle	Arrosage
Nut	Écrou
Oil can	Burette
Padlock	Cadenas
Plastic coated wire	Fil métallique plastifé

Pressure washer	Nettoyeur à haute-pression
Profile	Profilé
Rake	Râteau
Rope	Cordage
Satellite dish	Antenne parabolique
Screws	Vis
Shelf	Étagère
Sieve	Tamis
Spyhole	Judas optique
Staple nail	Crampillon
Storage box	Coffre de rangement
Striker plate	Gâche

Suction pump	Pompe vide-cave
Tarpaulin	Bâche
Wall plug	Cheville de fixation
Washer metal	Rondelle
Washer rubber	Joint caoutchouc

JOINERY
MENUISERIE

Bannister	**Balustre**
Blinds	**Stores**
Door & frame	**Bloc-porte**
Loft ladder	**Escalier escamotable**
Roof window	**Fenêtre de toit**
Shutter	**Volet**

Stairs
  circular
  straight
  turning
	Escaliers
	hélicoïdal
	droit
	tournant

Windows wood/pvc	**Fenêtres** bois/pvc

KITCHEN
CUISINE

Edging strip	Bande de chant
Hob	Plaque de cuisson
ceramic	céramique
gas	gaz
Junction strip	Profil de jonction
Kitchen units	Meuble de cuisine
Melamine strip	Feuille de mélaminé
Mixer tap single lever	Mitigeur
Mixer tap twin lever	Mélangeur
Sealing strip	Joint d'étanchéité

Sink	Évier
Sink cabinet	Meuble sous évier
Sink double	Évier deux cuve
Sink worktop	Évier à encastrer
Trim	Profil de finition
Waste disposal	Broyeur sanitaire
Worktop	Plan de travail

LIGHTING
ÉCLAIRAGE

Ceiling lights	Plafonnier
Flood light	Projecteur
Infrared detector	Détecteur infrarouge
Lead light	Baladeuse
Light bulb	Ampoule

Lighting
   external
   interior
	Éclairage
	extérieur
	intérieur

Programmer	Programmateur
Solar light	Balise solaire
Spot light recessed	Spot à encastrer
Spot surface mounted	Spot en saillie

Strip light	Réglette
Torch	Torche
Wall light	Applique
Workshop light	Éclairage de chantier

PAINTING/DECORATING
PEINTURE/DÉCORATION

Anti-fungal	Anti-mousse
Borders decorative	Frises
Ceiling rose	Rosace
Extension pole	Perche télescopique
Filler	Enduit de rebouchage
Filler finishing	Enduit de lissage
Float	Lisseuse/platoir
Glue	Colle
Masking tape	Rubane de masquage
Mastic	Mastic
Metal paint	Peinture fer

Mortar	Mortier
Paint	Peinture
Paint brush	Pinceau
Paint stripper gun	Décapeur
Paint tray	Bac à peinture
Paper roller	Roulette de colleur
Plaster	Plâtre
Plastic sheeting	Bâche plastique
Plumb bob/Plumline	Fil à plomb
Reinforcing tape	Caliquot adhésif
Roller	Rouleau
Roller handle	Monture

Roller sleeve	Manchon
Rust treatment	Traitment antirouille
Sandpaper	Papier de verre
Scraper	Couteau de peintre
Sealant	Étanche
Stencil	Pochoir
Textured coating	Crépi
Undercoat	Sous-couche
Varnish	Vernis
Wallpaper	Papier peint
Wire brush	Brosse métallique
Wood paint	Peinture bois

| Wood stain | Lasure |
| Wood treatment | Traitment bois |

PATIO
TERRASSE

Awning	Store
manual	manuel
motorised	motorisée
Balustrade	Balustre
Blocks	Pavés
Decking	Terrasse en bois
Fencing	Clôture
panel	panneau
wire	grillage
wood, treated	bois, traité
Gates	Portails
aluminium	aluminium
iron	fer
Paving slabs	Dalles
Remote control	Télécommand

PLUMBING
PLOMBERIE

Compression type	Union bicône
Copper tube	Tube cuivre
Elbow	Coude
Fittings	Raccords
brass	laiton
copper	cuivre
screw	visser
solder	souder
Flexible connector	Flexible raccord
Jointing paste	Pâte à joint
Jointing thread	Filasse
Nipple	Mamelon
Olive	Olive
Pipe clips	Collier de fixation

Plug sink	Bouchon de bonde
Stop cock	Robinet d'arrêt
Stop end (pipe)	Bouchon
Straight connector	Manchon
Tap washer	Joint de robinet
Tee	Té
Trap	Siphon
Valve	Vanne
Washer fibre	Joint fibro
Washer rubber	Joint caoutchouc
Waste pipe fitting	Evacuation de l'eau
Water heater	Chauffe-eau

WC flush mechanism

**Mécanismes
WC complet**

PROTECTIVE CLOTHING
VÊTEMENTS DE PROTECTION

Dust mask	Masque antipoussière
Ear plugs	Bouchons d'oreilles
Ear protectors	Casque anti-bruit
Eye protectors (goggles)	Lunettes de protection
Face mask	Masque respiratoire
Hard hat	Casque de chantier
High vis.jacket	Gilet de signalisation fluorescent
Knee pads	Genouillères

Lumbar support	Ceinture de maintien lombaire
Visor	Visière de protection
Work gloves	Gants travaux

SECURITY
SÉCURITÉ

Alarm wireless	Alarme sans fil
Camera surveillance	Caméra surveillance
Doorbell	Sonnette
Electric garage door	Automatisme portail de garage
Electric gate opener	Motorisation portail
Intercom	Interphone
Lock electric	Serrure électrique
Mortice lock	Serrure à mortaiser
Motion detector	Détecteur de mouvement

Remote control	**Télécommande**
Smoke detector	**Détecteur de fumée**

TILES
CARRELAGE

Border tile	Listel
Finishing trim	Baguette
Float	Lisseuse/Platoir
Float/toothed	Platoire /dentelle
Floor tile	Carrelage sol
Grout	Joint
Render	Ragréage
Rubber hammer	Maillet caoutchouc
Screed	Chape
Spacers	Croisillons
Spreader	Peigne à colle

Squeegee	Raclette caoutchouc

Tile adhesive
  ready mixed
  powder
	Colle
	en pâte
	en poudre

Tile cutter	Coupe tuile
Tile cutter/electric	Coup carreux /électrique
Wall tiles	Faïence mural

TIMBER
BOIS DE CHARPENTE

Beam	Poutre
Chipboard	Aggloméré
Fascia board	Planche de rive

Finished panels
   melamine
   solid
	Tablette
	mélaminée
	massif

Flooring	Dalles
Mouldings	Moulures
Panelling	Lambris
Planed	Rabotée
Plank	Planche
Plywood	Contreplaqué
Sawn	Brut

Sheets	Panneaux
Skirting	Plinthe
Timber lengths	
small section	tasseau
medium section	bastaing
large section	madrier
Tongue/groove	Rainure/ languette
Water resistant	Hydrofuge

TOOLS
OUTILLAGE

Adhesive spreader	Peigne à colle
Adjustable spanner	Clé à molette
Allen keys	Clé à sixpans
Angle grinder	Meuleuse d'angle
Arc welder	Souder à l'arc
Blow lamp	Lampe à souder
Blow torch	Chalumeau
Bucket	Seau
Chalk line	Cordeau craie
Chisel wood	Ciseau à bois
Circular saw	Scie circulaire

Clamp	Pince de serrage
Cleaver	Merlin
Club Hammer	Massette
Compressor	Compresseur
Concrete spreader	Epandeur à béton
Cutting disc	Disque à tronçonner
Drill (cordless)	Perceuse (sans fil)

Drills
  masonary
  metal
  wood
	Forets
	béton
	métaux
	bois

File	Lime
Float	Lisseuse/Platoir

Gas cartridge	Cartouche butane
Generator	Groupe électrogène
Hammer	Marteau
Hammer drill	Perceuse à percussion
Hand saw	Scie égoine
Hoist	Palan
Hole cutter	Scie cloche
Jig saw	Scie sauteuse
Ladder	Échelle
Laser level	Niveau laser
Measure (tape) long short	Mesure longue courte-ruban

Measure (ultra sonic)	Mesure ultra-sons
Mitre box	Boîte à coupe
Mitre saw	Scie à onglet
Paint spray gun	Pistolet à peinture
Pick-axe	Pioche
Pincher	Tenaille
Pipe cutter	Coupe-tube
Plane	Rabot
Plane electric	Rabot électrique
Pliers	Pinces
Pneumatic tools	Outils pneumatiques
Rasp	Râpe

Respiratory mask	Masque respiratoire
Retractable knife	Couteau lame rétractable
Rodding wire	Déboucheur flexible
Router	Défonceuse
Rubber hammer	Maillet caoutchouc
Sack barrow	Diable
Sander	Ponceuse
Scaffold	Échafaudage
Scissors	Paire de ciseaux
Screwdriver	Tournevis
Screwdriver bit	Embout

Screwdriver electric	Tournevis sans fil
Set square	Équerre de menuisier
Shovel	Pelle
Sink plunger	Ventouse à manche
Sledge hammer	Masse
Socket set	Coffret à douilles
Solder iron	Fer à souder
Spade	Bêche
Spanner	Clé
Spirit level	Niveau à bulle
Stapler	Agrafeuse
Stapler/nailer	Agrafeuse /cloueuse

Stepladder	Escabeau
Stillson wrench	Clé serre-tube stillson
Straight edge	Règle de maçon
Tenon saw	Scie à dos
Tile cutter	Coupe - carreaux
Tool box	Boîte de rangement
Trestle	Tréteau
Trowel	Truelle
Vice	Étau
Work bench/folding	Établi pliant

Alphabetical-Alphabétique

Adhesive spreader	Peigne à colle
Adjustable spanner	Clé à molette
Aerial	Antenne
Air conditioning	Climatisation
Air vent	Grilles d'aération
Alarm wireless	Alarme sans fil
Allen keys	Clé à sixpans
Angle bracket	Équerre d'assemblage
Angle grinder	Meuleuse d'angle
Anti-fungal	Anti-mousse
Arc welder	Souder à l'arc
Awning	Store
Backing box	Boîte d'encastrement
Ballast	Gravier
Balustrade	Balustre
Bannister	Balustre
Bath	Baignoire
Bathroom cabinet	Meuble de salle de bain
Bathroom panel	Tablier
Battery	Pile

Battery charger	Chargeur de pile
Beam	Poutre
Bend	Coude
Bitumen	Bitume
Bleed valve	Purgeur d'air
Blinds	Stores
Blocks concrete	Parpaings
Blocks (glass)	Briques de verre
Blocks (patio)	Pavés
Blow lamp	Lampe à souder
Blow torch	Chalumeau
Boiler	Chaudière
Bolt	Boulon
Borders decorative	Frises
Border tile	Listel
Bucket	Seau
Bulb	Ampoule
Bulb holder	Douille
Bungee	Sandow
Cable	Câble
flexible	souple
rigid	rigide
steel	acier
Cable tensioner	Tendeur oeil/croche

Camera surveillance	Caméra surveillance
Carpet	Moquette
Ceiling lights	Plafonnier
Ceiling rail	Fourrure
Ceiling rose	Rosace
Cement	Ciment
Chain	Chaîne
Chalk line	Cordeau craie
Chimney pipe	Tuyau de cheminée
Chimney sweep kit	Kit ramonage
Chipboard	Aggloméré
Chisel/wood	Ciseau à bois
Circuit breaker	Coup-circuit
Circular saw	Scie circulaire
Cistern	Réservoir
Clamp	Pince de serrage
Cleaver	Merlin
Clip	Mousqueton
Clip system	Clipser
Club hammer	Massette
Compression type	Union bicône
Compressor	Compresseur
Concrete mixer	Bétonnière
Concrete spreader	Epandeur à béton

Conduit	Gaine
Connecting strip	Barrette de connexion
Convector	Convecteur
Cooker hood	Hotte de cuisine
Copper tube	Tube cuivre
Corrugated sheets	Plaques ondulée
Crowbar	Pince à decoffrer
Curtain rod	Barre à rideaux
Cutting disc	Disque à tronçonner
Damp-proof membrane	Film sous dalle
Decking	Terrasse en bois
Door bars	Barre de seuil
Door bell	Sonnette
Door & frame	Bloc-porte
Door stop	Butée de porte
Double sided tape	Double face bande
Downpipe	Tuyau de descente

Drain rod	Déboucheur canalisation
Draught excluder	Isolation thermique
Drawing pin	Punaise
Drill (cordless)	Perceuse (sans fil)
Drills	Forets
masonary	béton
metal	métaux
wood	bois
Duck board	Caillebotis
Dustbin	Poubelle
Dust mask	Masque antipoussière
Ear plugs	Bouchons d'oreilles
Ear protectors	Casque anti-bruit
Edge bar	Barre d'arrêt
Edging strip	Bande de chant
Elbow	Coude
Electric garage door	Automatisme portail de garage
Electric gate opener	Motorisation portail

Electric heating	Chauffage électrique
Electric radiator	Panneau rayonnant
Expansion joints	Joint de dilatation
Extension cable	Rallonge
Extension lead	Enrouler de câble
Extension pole	Perche télescopique
Extension socket (anti surge)	Bloc (parafoudre)
Exterior door	Porte d'entrée
Eye protectors (goggles)	Lunettes de protection
Face mask	Masque respiratoire
Fan ventilation	Aérateur
Fascia board	Planche de rive
Fencing	Clôture
Fibre glass	Laine de verre
Fibre washer	Joint fibro
File	Lime
Filler	Enduit de rebouchage
Finished flooring	Parquet

Finished panel	Tablette
Finishing trim	Baguette
Fire guard	Pare-feu
Fittings	Raccords
Flashing/lead	Bande de plomb
Flexible connector	Flexible raccord
Float	Lisseuse/Platoir
Float/toothed	Platoir dentelle
Flood light	Projecteur
Floorboard	Plancher
Flooring	Dalles
Flooring ratchet strap	Sangle de serrage
Floor tile	Carrelage sol
Folding door	Porte pliante
Foot scraper	Caillebotis
Free-standing heaters	Chauffage d'appoint
Fuse box	Tableau électrique
Gas cartridge	Cartouche butane
Gate	Portail
Generator	Groupe électrogène
Glass blocks	Briques de verre

Glue	Colle
Grease separator	Séparateur à graisse
Grout	Joint
Gutter	Gouttière
Gutter clip	Crochet de gouttière
Gutter guard	Crapaudine
Hammer	Marteau
Hammer drill	Perceuse à percussion
Hand basin	Lave-main
Handles	Poignées
Hand saw	Scie égoïne
Hard hat	Casque de chantier
Heated towel rail	Sèche-serviette
High vis.jacket	Gilet de signalisation fluorescent
Hinge	Charnière
Hob	Plaque de cuisson
Hoist	Palan
Hole cutter	Scie cloche
Hook	Crochet
Hose	Tuyau

Hose reel	Dévidoir
Infrared detector	Détecteur infrarouge
Inspection chambers	Regards
Insulating tape	Ruban isolant
Intercom	Interphone
Internal door	Porte intérieur
Jacuzzi bath	Baignoire balnéo
Jerrycan	Jerrycan
Jet head	Lance à jet
Jig saw	Scie sauteuse
Joint	Jonction
Jointing paste	Pâte à joint
Jointing tape	Bande pour joint
Jointing thread	Filasse
Jubilee clip	Collier de serrage
Junction box	Boîte de derivation
Junction strip	Profil de jonction
Junction strip/floor	Barre de jonction
Key	Clé

Kitchen units	Meuble de cuisine
Knee pads	Genouillères
Ladder	Échelle
Laminate	Sol stratifié
Laser level	Niveau laser
Lead light	Baladeuse
Letter box	Boîte aux lettres
Lifting door	Porte basculante
Light bulb	Ampoule
Lighting	Éclairage
inside	intérieur
outside	extérieur
Lino	Linoleum
Lock	Verrou
Lock electric	Serrure électrique
Loft ladder	Escalier escamotable
Lubricants	Lubrifiantes
Lumbar support	Ceinture de maintien lombaire
Macerater	Broyeur
Masking tape	Rubane de masquage

Mastic	Mastic
Measure (tape)	Mesure
long	longue
short	courte-ruban
Measure (ultra sonic)	Mesure ultra-sons
Melamine strip	Feuille de melamine
Metal paint	Peinture fer
Metal sheeting	Plaque métal
Metal stud frame	Rail de cloisons
Mirror	Miroir
Mitre box	Boîte à coupe
Mitre saw	Scie à onglet
Mixer tap single lever	Mitigeur
Mixer tap twin lever	Mélangeur
Mortar	Mortier
Mortice lock	Serrure à mortaiser
Motion detector	Détecteur de mouvement
Motorised	Motorisée
Moulding	Moulure
Nail	Clou
Nipple	Mamelon

Nozzle	Arrosage
Nut	Écrou
Oil can	Burette
Oil filled radiator	Radiateur chaleur douce à fluide
Olive	Olive
Padlock	Cadenas
Paint	Peinture
Paint brush	Pinceau
Paint spray gun	Pistolet à peinture
Paint stripper gun	Décapeur
Paint tray	Bac à peinture
Panelling	Lambris
Paper roller	Roulette de colleur
Paving slabs	Dalles
Pedal bin	Poubelle à pédale
Pick-axe	Pioche
Pincher	Tenaille
Pipe clip	Collier de fixation
Pipe cutter	Coupe-tube
Pivoting door	Porte pivotante

Plane	Rabot
Planed	Rabotée
Plane electric	Rabot électrique
Plank	Planche
Plaster	Plâtre
Plaster board	Plaque de plâtre
Plaster board screws	Vis plaque de plâtre
Plastic coated wire	Fil métallique plastifé
Plasticiser	Résine latex
Plastic sheeting	Bâche plastique
Pliers	Pinces
Plug (sink)	Bouchon de bonde
Plug electric	Prise de courant
two pin	fiche mâle
Plumb bob/Plumline	Fil à plomb
Plywood	Contreplaqué
Pneumatic tools	Outils pneumatique
Polycarbonate roofing	Plaques polycarbonate

Pressure washer	Nettoyeur à haute- pression
Profile	Profilé
Programmer	Programmateur
Prop	Étais
Pump	Circulateur
Radiator	Radiateur
Rake	Râteau
Rasp	Râpe
Reinforcing rods	Fer à béton
Reinforcing tape	Caliquot adhésif
Remote control	Télé-commande
Render	Ragréage
Respiratory mask	Masque respiratoire
Retractable knife	Couteau lame rétractable
Rockwool	Laine de roche
Rodding wire	Déboucheur flexible
Roller	Rouleau
Roller handle	Monture
Roof window	Fenêtre de toit
Rope	Cordage
Router	Défonceuse

Rubber hammer	Maillet caoutchouc
Rust treatment	Traitement antirouille
Sack barrow	Diable
Sand	Sable
Sander	Ponceuse
Sandpaper	Papier de verre
Satellite dish	Antenne parabolique
Sawn	Brut
Scaffold	Échafaudage
Scissors	Paire de ciseaux
Scraper	Couteau de peintre
Screed	Chape
Screw	Vis
Screwdriver	Tournevis
Screwdriver bit	Embout
Screwdriver cordless	Tournevis sans fil
Sealant	Étanche
Sealing strip	Joint d'étanchéité
Septic tank	Fosse septique

Service door	Porte de service
Set square	Équerre de menuisier
Sheets	Panneaux
Shelf	Étagère
Shovel	Pelle
Shower	Douche
Shower curtain	Rideau de douche
Shower enclosure	Parois de douche
Shower kit	Ensemble de douche
Shower tray	Receveur
Shutter	Volet
Sieve	Tamis
Sink	Évier
Sink cabinet	Meuble sous évier
Sink plunger	Ventouse à manche
Sink worktop	Évier à encastrer
Skirting	Plinthe
Sledge hammer	Masse
Sliding door	Porte coulissante
Solar light	Balise solaire

Smoke detector	Détecteur de fumée
Socket/ waterproof	Prise/ étanche
Socket set	Coffret à douilles
Solder iron	Fer à souder
Sound insulation	Isolation phonique
Spacers	Croisillons
Spade	Bêche
Spanner	Clé
Spirit level	Niveau à bulle
Spot light recessed	Spot à encastrer
Spot surface mounted	Spot en saillie
Spreader	Peigne à colle
Spyhole	Judas optique
Squeegee	Raclette caoutchouc
Stairs	Escaliers
Stapler	Agrafeuse
Staple nail	Crampillons
Stapler/nailer	Agrafeuse/ cloueuse
Stencil	Pochoir
Stepladder	Escabeau
Stillson wrench	Clé serre-tube stillson
Stop cock	Robinet d'arrêt

Stop end (gutter)	Fond gouttière
Stop end (pipe)	Bouchon
Storage box	Coffre de rangement
Stove/built in	Foyer/Insert
Stove freestanding	Poêle à bois
Straight connector	Manchon
Straight edge	Règle de maçon
Striker plate	Gâche
Strip light	Réglette
Suction pump	Pompe vide-cave
Switch	Interrupteur
Switch(two way)	Va-et-vient
Tap	Robinet
Tap washer	Joint de robinet
Tarpaulin	Bâche
Tee	Té
Tenon saw	Scie à dos
Test meter	Appareil de mesure
Textured coating	Crépi
Thermostat	Thermostat
Tile adhesive	Colle
Tile cutter	Coupe tuile
Timber lengths	Bois
small section	tasseau
medium section	bastaing
large section	madrier

Toilet	Toilette
Toilet bowl	Cuvette WC
Toilet brush holder	Pot à balai
Toilet roll holder	Dérouleur de papier WC
Toilet seat	Abattant WC
Tongue/groove	Rainure/ languette
Tool box	Boîte de rangement
Torch	Torche
Towel rail	Porte-serviette
Trap	Siphon
Trestle	Tréteau
Trim	Profil de finition
Trowel	Truelle
Undercoat	Sous-couche
Underlay	Sous-couche
Valve	Vanne
Varnish	Vernis
Vent	Grille d'aération
Ventilator unit	VMC (ventilation mécanique contrôle)
Vermiculite	Vermiculite
Vertical wall rail	Montant
Vice	Étau

Visor	Visière de protection
Wall hung WC	WC suspendu
Wall light	Applique
Wallpaper	Papier peint
Wall plug	Cheville fixation
Wall tiles	Faïence mural
Wash basin/stand	Lavabo
Wash bowl	Vasque
Washer metal	Rondelle
Washer rubber	Joint caoutchouc
Waste disposal	Broyeur
Waste pipe fitting	Evacuation de l'eau
Water heater	Chauffe-eau
Water resistant	Hydrofuge
WC flush mechanism	Mécanisme WC complet
Wheel barrow	Brouette
Window	Fenêtre
Wire	Fil
Wire brush	Brosse métallique
Wood fire	Feu de bois
Wood paint	Peinture bois
Wood stain	Lasure
Wood treatment	Traitement bois
Work bench/folding	Établi/pliant

Work gloves	Gants travaux
Workshop light	Éclairage de chantier
Worktop	Plan de travail

WEIGHTS AND MEASURES
POIDS ET MESURES

LINEAR MEASURES -   MESURES DE
                                   LONGUEUR

SQUARE MEASURES -   MESURES DE
                                   SUPERFICIE

CUBIC MEASURES   -   MESURES DE
                                   VOLUME

WEIGHTS   -   POIDS

LINEAR MEASURES - MESURES DE LONGUEUR

British system

1 Inch (pouce)	2.54cm
1 Foot (pied)	30.48cm
1 Yard (yard)	91.44cm
1 Furlong (furlong)	201.17m
1 Mile (mile)	1.609km

Metric system

1 Millimètre (mm)	0.03937 inch
1 Centimètre (cm)	0.3937 inch
1 Mètre (m)	39.37 inches
1 Kilomètre (km)	0.6214 mile

SQUARE MEASURES - MESURES DE SUPERFICIE

British system

1 in2 (pouce carré)	6.45 cm2
1 ft2 (pied carré)	929.03 cm2
1 yd2 (yard carré)	0.836 m2
1 acre	0.4047 ha

Metric system

1 cm2	0.155 in2
1 m2	1.196 yd2
1 km2	0.3861 Ml2
1 ha	2.471 acres

CUBIC MEASURES - MESURES DE VOLUME

British system

1 in3 (pouce cube)	16.387 cm3
1 ft3 (pied cube)	0.028 m3
1 yd3 (yard cube)	0.765 m3

Metric system

1 cm3	0.061 in3
1m3	1.308 yd3
1 litre (1000 cm3)	1.76 pints

NOTE firewood is often sold by the 'stère'
1 stère is equal to 1 cubic metre.

WEIGHTS – POIDS

British system

1 Ounce (once)	28.349gm
1 Pound (livre)	453.59gm
1 Stone	6.348kg
1 Ton	1.016 tonne

Metric system

1 kg	2.2046 lb
1 tonne	0.9842 ton

MISCELLANEOUS - MISCELLANÉES

AMBULANCE		**SAMU**
RING	**15**	
FIRE BRIGADE		**POMPIERS**
RING	**18**	
POLICE		**POLICE**
RING	**17**	

EMERGENCY EUROPE
APPEL URGENCES EUROPÉEN

RING 112